Dedication

For Alex

You came into my life and changed everything in an instant. You came in quietly, completely and in ways that I never expected.

By the time you arrived, I thought I had already learned so many of life's big lessons about motherhood, my identity and how to surrender. But you, Alex, over the years, have become my greatest teacher.

Your lessons were & still are different. They are deeper and woven into the quietest moments, the toughest days; especially in those frustrating communication breakdowns between us, and in every single triumph we've had, no matter how small they seemed to others.

Even in your silence, you spoke, with your eyes, your presence, your spirit. You taught me to truly and authentically love without conditions. To let go of any expectations I had, even when that continues to feel challenging, and to find joy in what others may overlook.

You've shaped not only the mother I am, but the work I do and the person I'm still becoming.

You showed me my purpose.
You lit a fire within me and changed my view of the world.

Thank you for teaching, guiding, and growing me every single day.

With all my love, always,

Mum
xoxo

Why won't you fucking speak?

Written by Tash Howlett

Copyright © 2025 - Tash Talks Communication

All rights reserved. No part of this book may be reproduced in any manner whatsoever without prior written permission of the publisher.

First Printing, 2025

Published by Tash Talks Communication
www.tashhowlett.com

Hardcover
ISBN 978-1-7640982-3-6

Paperback
ISBN 978-1-7640982-4-3

eBook
ISBN 978-1-7640982-8-1

The nights are quiet with stars so bright,
the world is peaceful, but we can't sleep.
We've waited so long for those first words,
wondering, why won't you fucking speak?

The playgrounds a buzz with chatter and cheer,
but your words are missing, so silent and meek.
We listen deeper for that one whisper, or sound,
why won't you fucking speak?

Other kids babble, they chatter and laugh,
as their words fill the air.
We stay in silence, our hearts still aching,
asking, why won't you fucking speak?

Our nights are long and sleepless,
as we dream of the words you'll say.
But, the morning comes, you're still quiet,
and the time keeps slipping away.
Yearning, why won't you fucking speak?

Our frustration builds, the anger grows,
we rage at life, at fate, and sometimes you.
Why can't you say something.... anything?
Pleading, why won't you fucking speak?

We grieve the dreams we have for you,
the milestones, the talks, the play.
We mourn the words we have never heard,
and the ones that you might not say.

But then we start to see a look, a laugh,
or a little whisper that is so uniquely you.
We start to recognise, maybe you are speaking,
just not in the way that we knew.

Your eyes tell stories and hands express,
your spark, your needs, and love so deep.
We begin to hear you, in unexpected ways,
maybe, you don't need to fucking 'speak'!

Our dreams for you begin to change,

as the grief fades and we no longer weep.

We embrace the way that you tell your truth,

it's beautiful, even if you never 'speak'.

In the quiet, we find our peace,
your voice is strong and true.
You speak in ways we never thought,
and we're so damn proud of you!

So here we are, no longer waiting,

not begging for that one small peek.

We hear you; we love you, exactly as you are.

You are perfect, EVEN IF you NEVER fucking 'speak'!

To the parents, carers, or loved ones,
who have ever thought, whispered, screamed, or silently wept, "why won't you fucking speak?"

This book is for you!

For the intense love that we share as we transition through the constant 'silence'.

For the grief & guilt that we may feel, while also feeling the endless amounts of gratitude.

For the somewhat messy, yet spectacular truth that we can fiercely and wholeheartedly accept our children, whether they speak with words, with gestures, or any other mode of communication, as we process our own grief of the dreams we once held tight.

There is no wrong in feeling both of these contrasting feelings.
There shouldn't be any reason to feel shame in OUR longing for what we thought we were 'getting', just as our love is never-ending and has no boundaries.

We are our loved ones' fiercest protectors as we navigate the advocating..... in the waiting rooms, against the systems, fighting for inclusion and also holding space when the world feels too loud, too small &/or too 'exclusive'.

Let this book be a reminder of one aspect of our truth, which is rarely spoken due to the shame and judgments often projected toward our experiences. This is a reminder that these contrasting feelings can, in fact, coexist, and that by honouring OUR own story, we do not in any way take away anything from theirs.

We need to remember that we are not alone when navigating this journey.

We are not broken, just as much as they are not either.

And we are never too much!

www.ingramcontent.com/pod-product-compliance
Lightning Source LLC
Chambersburg PA
CBHW041110070526
44583CB00003B/130